Songwrit and Melody Writing for Beginners:

How to Become a Songwriter in 24 Hours or Less!

By: Alexander Wright

(Alexander Wright) Copyright © 2015

All rights reserved. No part of this book may be reproduced in any form without permission in writing from the author. Portions of this book's content can be used only if properly referenced.

Disclaimer

No part of this publication may be reproduced or transmitted in any form or by any means, mechanical or electronic, including photocopying or recording, or by any information storage and retrieval system, or transmitted by email without permission in writing from the publisher. While all attempts and efforts have been made to verify the information held within this publication, neither the author nor the publisher assumes any responsibility for errors, omissions, or opposing interpretations of the content herein.

This book is for entertainment purposes only. The views expressed are those of the author alone, and should not be taken as expert instruction or commands. The reader of this book is responsible for his or her own actions when it comes to reading the book. Adherence to all applicable laws and regulations, including international, federal, state, and local governing professional licensing, business practices, advertising, and all other aspects of doing business in the US, Canada, or any other jurisdiction is the sole responsibility of the purchaser or reader.

Neither the author nor the publisher assumes any responsibility or liability whatsoever on the behalf of the purchaser or reader of these materials. Any received slight of any individual or organization is purely unintentional.

Table of Contents

Introduction

Introduction to Songwriting

Chapter 1 - Do Your Homework

Chapter 2- The Chicken or the Egg

Chapter 3- Writing Your Lyrics

Chapter 4- Writing Your Melody

Chapter 5- Finalizing Your Song

Songwriter's Checklist

Conclusion

Check Out My Other Books

Introduction

First and foremost I want to thank you for downloading the book, "Songwriting: Lyric and Melody Writing for Beginners: How to Become a Songwriter in 24 Hours or Less!"

In this book, you will not only learn how to write lyrics, but you'll also learn about creating a melody that will hold the song together. From this book, you will learn how to choose a genre, how to get started writing your song, the significance of a song title, how to craft a catchy hook, the basics of song structure, and ultimately, how to write a song in 24 hours or less!

Thanks again for downloading this book! I hope you enjoy it, and please leave a review once you are finished.

Introduction to Songwriting

Literally all cultures have evidence of some shape or form of music. Music varies widely, and in as technology advances, so does music. Music can hardly even be defined with one solid phrase nowadays because of the rate that it's evolving. Most can agree, however, that music is generally described as a fine art that utilizes sound and silence to produce a rhythmic melody. Music is often accompanied by a voice, but not all music involves singing. Since its speculated origination well over 50,000 years ago, it has become ingrained in every single human culture around the world. There is not a single known civilization that did not use music for at least one purpose. Music can change your mood, relax your mind, assist with physical exertion, inspire minds, communicate feelings, and do so much more - music truly has an endless list of applications.

So you sit down to write a lyrical master masterpiece with an entrancing melody. Perhaps when you first sit down, you can manage to jot down a few nice lines or a few chords. You feel like it's really going great. Then, after two hours or so you look at your beautiful work, and realize you've only written down two sentences. Writing music is not something that people are just born with - if you're having issues getting what's in your head onto paper and into notes, that's perfectly fine. It's normal. To create a song, you have to know certain things, exercise patience, and be prepared to sit down for a while. Writing music is definitely not a walk in the park, but with the help of this book, you'll be writing music in 24 hours or less.

Do Your Homework

The first step for any major project is to do your research. You can never research any subject too much. Music is such a vast art, and there are hundreds of genres and even more sub-genres. You may or may not have noticed, but every day it seems there is a new genre popping up on radios or on the internet. This is both good and bad for you as an aspiring songwriter. More genres mean that you have more styles to express yourself in, and a wider range of variety is always healthy. The bad news is, this means more research for you. A lot more. You may already know what your favorite genre is, but you never know what form your song will flourish in. You need to experiment a little and see which fits your style of writing music. Every single musician has a 'mood' that is associated with their songs. Sometimes you'll come across a famous band that is well known now and look back at some of their earliest songs. Their style may have been much different when the band originated, and it generally seems that the artists just couldn't express themselves in their old genre. When the find the perfect fit, however, they can skyrocket to the top of the lists. The problem isn't that they didn't know how to write, it's that they were focusing their effort in all the wrong places. To avoid this and to write the best song you possibly can, a few hours of research are first needed.

The first step you should take when researching musical genres is to just listen to a bunch of songs such as: John Legend, Elvis Presley, Prince, Stevie Wonder, Bob Dylan, Carrie Underwood, and even Dr. Dre. Listen to the widest variety of music that you can, regardless of how much you despise the genre or hate the artist. You need to analyze all the songs that you can in order to make one yourself. Songwriting is an art, and people often forget that art takes time to master. Looking at other masterpieces is a great way to learn quickly. Even if you personally don't like the song, there is a reason that the songwriter is famous, so study as many songs as possible. Look at the lyrics. Some songs have funny lyrics, just made to make listeners laugh. Others take on a more serious note, expressing the writer's deepest, innermost emotions. Observe usage of things like rhyming, similes, allusions, idioms, and other figures of speech. Often times, words will be slightly modified to fit in with the tempo or melody of a song. Sometimes this can sound cheesy and inorganic if not done correctly, so take note of how popular songs do this effectively. Look at things like pauses and line breaks. A pause in music is when a song temporarily comes to a complete stop and then resumes. A line break is when a line of text is divided and has absolutely no effect on the sound of your song. Line breaks are used purely to give poetic meaning and deeper sentiment to lyrics. Make sure to discern certain songwriters' styles, and look for identifiable patterns. When you're writing your own song, don't just copy their style; use it to make your own, unique style. Unique style and creativity is what makes a song special. After you look into the words and find their true meaning, take a look at popular songs' melodies. Again, don't stick to one genre of music at this point, because if you do you're only hurting your ability to write a great song. There are fast paced songs with few words, slow songs that are mostly singing, and other songs that feature rapping, which is technically a mixture of poetry and speech, not singing. These little things are going to become so very important to you as you learn the ways of songwriting. After you spend some time researching the lyrics of several genres, you need to look at the tune, rhythm, beats, and melody. There are some generalizations that can be made about a song based on its genre. If it's a country song, you can expect some sort of stringed instrument, as this is common in many country songs. A rock song will likely feature an electric guitar. Songs from the pop and hip-hop genres will likely have more computerized melodies. While this may not be true for every song in its genre, making generalizations such as these can help you decide what genre your song will be.

Once you have all that research down, you're going to want to decide on your genre. This particular step is important because it will lay down the foundation for the melody and lyrics in the future. Knowing your genre before you start choosing a tempo will save time and eliminate a lot of confusion. This also means that you can do even more research, this time with a much smaller variety of songs. Let's say that you've decided that your song will be in the Country Blues genre, then you need to listen to musicians that are talented in that field such as: Alger Texas Alexander, Lightnin' Hopkins, Blind Willie Johnson, and John Lee Hooker. During this phase of development, avoid listening to other, unrelated songs if you can help it. Try not to listen to Kanye West, Led Zeppelin, or Taylor Swift in the short time you're gathering your information. Listening to too many genres while you are trying to analyze songs for certain patterns may muddle your findings and ultimately lower the quality of your song. From your findings, you might notice that these famous country blues artists have a tendency to use harmonicas for a large portion of the melody. Take note of this, and prepare to include a harmonica into your country blues song. Perhaps you also notice how country blues songs are frequently used to tell real life stories. In this case, try to remember a funny, interesting, or weird experience from the past and think of how you can convert it into blues-like format. After this is all completed, you can begin the next step or creating your lyrical masterpiece.

The Chicken or the Egg?

Since famous naturalist Charles Darwin proposed the theory of evolution, it seems more questions were brought about then answers. Among these questions is the common query "Which came first, the chicken or the egg?" While the question still floats around still not positively answered, it can be likened to a number of situations. In our case, which comes first, the lyrics or the melody? If you start with lyrics will you get a better melody? Or should the melody be set down first to provide guidelines for your lyrics? You probably want a definite answer, correct? Unfortunately, just like the question of the day, there really is no absolute answer. Some biologists argue the egg must have come first as a mutation in a chicken-like bird. This is like the people that insist you must create your lyrics first, otherwise they will be meaningless. Then, you have the scientists that are on the complete other side of the spectrum asserting that you need to create a simple melody to use as a basis before you can add any words. Even still, there will be people swearing that the only way to write a song with both great lyrics and a catchy melody is to flip flop between the two, creating part of the melody, then part of the lyrics.

In the midst of all this chaos, I believe I've found the closest thing to an answer we'll ever find - it depends. It depends on you and what you prefer, it depends if you already have the lyrics, it depends if the genre your song will be is usually melody heavy, and it depends on so much more. Honestly, the only useful suggestion one can give is try both, and see which one you get the most out of. It's unfortunate that there is no real answer, but everyone is different. If you quickly write five chords and five lines, then alternate by writing five different lines and five chords, you will be able to see what works best for you.

If the answer above just can't satisfy your curiosity, then we'll look at some data. An online study conducted in 2013 asked songwriters to describe the steps they took in order to produce their music. While this doesn't give anyone a definite answer, it is certainly helpful to see how a majority of people do it. In regards to writing lyrics or creating a melody first, there really is no wrong way. It's all about preference. So what do more people prefer? More songwriters started by writing lyrics first. About 19 percent more, actually. While around 37% of songwriters preferred starting out with just lyrics, only approximately 18% decided that they liked having a melody before writing down any words. There were several other groups that decided to begin their songs by using other means, some of which we will discuss later. The largest group under those who prefer writing a melody first, with 16% of songwriters, said that it varies. This means that 16% of the surveyed songwriters change how they start writing their song every time they write a new one. Ultimately, more people like starting out with some words on paper. Supposedly it helps the melody fall in place more effectively. Even with the results from the poll, don't let this sway you. If you feel that the only way you can write a good song is by starting with a melody, then start putting some chords together, there's nothing wrong with that. Even if you like writing a portion of the lyrics first, then working on a few chords, that's okay. Whatever works best for you is what you should continue doing.

Writing Your Lyrics

Since the largest majority of people chose to start writing their songs with the lyrics, I'll explain this process first. Say that you, too, decide to write your lyrics before your melody. Great, you're now one step closer to producing your brilliant song. What's next? Well, write the lyrics! If only it were that simple, right? Luckily, with the help of this book, it can be. If you have no idea what to start with, a good pre-writing technique that can help you is free writing. Free writing is where all you do is write. It doesn't matter how stupid what you write sounds, how much you write, or even if there are grammatical errors. Free writing is used by many types of writers, and can be utilized by you as an aspiring songwriter. Sit down at a calm, quiet location, take out a pen and piece of paper, and just write. Set a time limit, no longer than thirty minutes, and tell yourself not to get up until the time is up. Writing in a notebook is better than using a computer or typing device because there is no autocorrect on a piece of paper. In the same sense, a pen is a better option than a pencil because you can't erase pen. Don't even pay attention to what you're writing, because then you may have the urge to revise it. This is a free write session, no editing is allowed. Not only does free writing get your flow going, but it can also give you some ideas for what to write your song about. If you sit down and prepare yourself for a free write session but can't seem to get anything down, you may need to get some inspiration. Read some poetry, listen to some music, and then try free writing again. After your time runs out and you have a significant amount of writing, look at it quickly and see if anything stands out. You may find three or four sentences you like; you might find a whole page you like. Even if you don't find anything useful, you still just defeated any writer's nemesis - writer's block.

 With writer's block out of the picture, and possibly some lines already written, you're going to want a title for your song. Writing a title for your song can be done before or after the rest of the lyrics, but it's most helpful to get one down first, even if it's just temporary. There are a few things that you should consider when writing a song title. First of all, you're going to want to make your audience curious. Make your listener wonder what the title means, but don't make it vague or cliché. Allow space for imagination, but don't leave your title unexplained. Your song title will also have to be memorable for people to keep listening to your song, and tell others about it. In the age of computers, phones, and search engines, most people will only be able to find new content through keywords. If you make your song title ridiculous and impossible to remember, nobody can discover your music. Another thing to remember when writing a title is that it's a title. It's not an introductory paragraph to your song, so don't treat it like one. A good practice is to keep your titles under five words. If it's absolutely necessary, your title may be five words, but in most cases six words just become overbearing. If you already have a hook in mind, that is a lyrical device that is repeated throughout the song to catch the listener's attention, then your title should be relevant to your hook. After all this consideration, your result should be an amazing, interesting, outstanding title that will draw people to listen to your song.

 The next step for writing your song is to write a hook. As it was previously explained, hooks are repeated constantly throughout a song. Hooks are supposed to be catchy and interesting so that the stick in listeners ears. Besides sounding nice, a hook has to make sense. A properly written hook holds the entire song together and gives a deeper meaning to each line. The hook is a very important part of any song. As such a vital part of your song, you need to make sure your hook is as good as it can be. You probably don't want to settle with a hook like "That's cool car." Your hook has to pull on the listener's' emotions. Vivid, descriptive hooks are necessary to make your song special. To get a sense of what a hook should be like, listen to some more music. To develop your song, you're going to have to go through a lot of steps that involve listening to music, because popular songs have, for the most part, all the elements you'll need for yours. While listening to music this time, however, only pay attention to the hooks of each song. Write some of your favorite ones down, and take note of how often each hook is repeated. It will also help you if you understand how hooks are utilized based on different genres. After you do this, sit down, and write a list of hooks relevant to the title or titles you have down. Select the best pair, and then it's time to move on.

This next step might remind you of a high school English class. You have your title, and you have your hook. These are arguably the most important part of a song. You can't just publish two lines and call it a song, however. You're going to need to fill your song with meaning, sentiment, and imagery, all while keeping it in a nice rhythm. Certain writers that deal with words have mastered this skill, without even utilizing a distinctive melody. These people are called poets. If you think about it, all music is is a poem with some extra noise. Some great poets for inspiration include most of the greats, like Shakespeare, Walt Whitman, Emily Dickinson, and Edgar Allen Poe. These are the names you probably heard in school. Venture deeper than your old textbook, however, and you'll find some real geniuses in the literary field. Some less common but equally amazing poets include John Donne, T. S. Eliot, and Rumi. Each poet has a personal style that can't be replicated, like Wallace Stevens simple and matter-of-factly tone. This is what sets them apart as great writers - their uniqueness. Don't try to steal their style, because you will fail, but at least learn from their expertise and attempt to craft your own persona.

    What makes many songs so well-known is their ability to communicate feelings from the songwriter to the listener. Adding sentiment into your lyrics will make them more memorable. When writing a song, you should first discern your reasoning. Why are you writing this song? Do you have a story to tell? What are you trying to achieve by writing this song? Asking yourself these questions is required to write a song that will touch other people's hearts. Delve deep into your aspirations, and find your driving force. Tap into whatever it is that gives you a reason to wake up every morning. The first thing you need to do in order to write meaningful lyrics is to find a topic that you can relate to. Find a topic that you honestly care about, and your audience will be able to feel the passion from the first few words, until the end. Don't just write a song about your last breakup because that's what's popular. A topic means more than just the contents of the song. A song should reflect your true feelings - don't be embarrassed to put your feelings all the way out there. You will have to learn how to express yourself freely if you want to write deep lyrics. One common mistake that those new to songwriting make is that every line has to rhyme. Forcing rhymes will make your lyrics weaker. Also, contrary to the popular belief, there is no universal law of songwriting that states you have to rhyme at least two lines in a row. Experiment with different techniques. Avoid writing down the first rhyme that comes to mind, as this word is very predictable. Reverting to the first rhyme you can think of will likely make your song sound boring.

You now should have inspiration from musicians and poets, and you also have a title and hook written down. You should also have a topic that means something to you. After all this research, you don't think that you'd have to more, correct? After all it is a song you're writing, not an essay, right? Unfortunately, that is the exact opposite of the correct answer. You can never do too much research in order to create a good song. What you have to look at next is something called song structure. Most songs have portions that repeat at different times, and these portions create the song structure. Included in the song structure are its components - the intro, verse, break, hook, bridge, chorus, and outro. None of these components have any specific positions, except for the intro and outro. An intro can only be placed at the beginning of a song, and an outro can only be at the end.

Not all songs have an intro, but an intro is a great way to initially draw people into a song. An intro is usually calmer than the main melody. In an intro, you can introduce concepts used throughout your song, and perhaps you can hint at your hook. Intros will very commonly lead into a verse. A verse is the 'flesh' of the song. Now that the intro has gotten the listener's attention give them something to remember. A verse generally isn't repeated, so you have to try to make an impression on the listener. Verses are most often stories that take the listener on a musical journey, and are split up by the other song structure components. Most of the time, this is where lyric writers will pour most of their own emotions into.

In between a verse, some songwriters may utilize something called a break. A break is essentially anything that interrupts the melody, not including a bridge. A break may be something like a solo, with just singing or just an instrument playing. Your song can also utilize silence as a break, to build up anticipation. Breaks aren't used as often as some of the other components, but they can add more dimension to your song if used correctly. Next comes your chorus. Your chorus needs to be well written, as this is the part of your song that repeats itself. A chorus is a group of multiple lines that repeat. Basically, choruses are used to sum up your entire song. If you believe your song doesn't have enough space for a chorus, you can use a refrain instead. A refrain is like a mini-chorus, in that it is only a single line in your song that repeats. The chorus repeats throughout a song, but isn't the same thing as your hook. A hook is usually made to be especially catchy, so that it 'hooks' your listener. Often times, if you have part of a song stuck in your head, it's because of the song's hook. Hooks often have lyrics that rhyme, display assonance, or are just fun to say. Finally, now that you have all these components down, it's time for you to say goodbye to your listeners. Outros aren't as commonly used as intros are, but they can be just as important. Your outro can finish the story your verse told, or it can leave them thinking.

Many popular songs today follow one of a few common song structures. Before we can really explore song structure, we have to understand the format that it is recorded in. Song structure is denoted by a letter in the alphabet. Each part of a song is assigned a specific letter. Generally, A is verse, B is the chorus, and C is the bridge. The most common song structure is the thirty two bar form, also known as the AABA form. This means that it would go Verse, Verse, Chorus, and Verse. The first verse, or 'A', of any song is usually the intro and is not differentiated from a verse. Hooks are most often placed at the opening and closing of each verse, but can be spread all over the place. Songs that exhibit this AABA format include the wildly popular Christmas song, "Deck the Halls"; the classic ballad sung by actress Judy Garland, "Somewhere Over the Rainbow"; and Led Zeppelin's "Whole Lotta Love". This song structure become extremely popular in the late 50's and hasn't lost its fame since. There is something particularly appealing about this certain song structure that people just seem to love. Other common song structures include the extremely simple AAA (verse/intro, verse, verse), ABAB (verse/intro, chorus, verse, chorus), and ABACAB (verse/intro, chorus, verse, bridge, verse, chorus). Remember that these don't include the outro or specify the position of every hook. After you decide what song structure will work best for you, then you can finally begin writing your lyrics. Keep in mind everything mentioned in this chapter, and your lyrics should hold substance and be catchy.

Writing Your Melody

If you followed the 37% of songwriters who start with the lyrics, you should have a large portion of your song finished. You're at the 50% mark, or right around there, anyway. The lyrics are a huge part of a song. They communicate verbally with your listeners and convey your thoughts directly. Don't overlook the impact of a nice melody though. Melodies alone can be stuck in a person's head for days, repeating over and over again until another song comes along and shoves it out. A good melody will provide a nice basis for your song, and it should hold your words together well. A melody is technically just a sequence of notes that sounds anything remotely like music. There is no order that you have to choose, no set number of beats per minute, and really no rules whatsoever. Writing a melody is difficult because of the vast amount of possibilities. Mathematically speaking, there are a near infinite amount of possible melodies you can choose, especially because a melody can be any length that you want it to be. While this means you don't have to worry about running out of music anytime soon, it definitely complicates the process of writing a memorable song. Soon enough, though, you'll be able to write an enjoyable melody without a problem.

Melodies are complicated. To put your feet in the water, so to speak, you should start exploring other melodies. If there is only one thing that you can take away from this book, it should be that you need to do a lot of research if you want to write a good song. Load up a few songs that you love and pay attention to how the melody supports the lyrics. Take notes, and then get experimenting. If you have a piano or keyboard, these are great for making quick and simple melodies. First, start with single notes, and then once you have a solid foundation of a melody, try transitioning to chords. Add some extra notes to fill in empty spaces, and progress from there. At this point, it would be smart for you to learn how to write and record music.

The treble clef, also known as the G clef, is the more common of the two clefs. When reading music, you read from left to right, bottom to top. On sheet music, it will be notated by the G-clef symbol, and is found above the F clef. A clef indicates the pitch of the musical notes that it contains. Notes are likened to syllables in the English language. They produce sound and are labeled by letters. The notes on the lines of the G clef are E, G, B, D, and F, from the bottom to the top. The spaces, which are in-between the lines, are F, A, C, and E. A good way to remember the lines of the G clef is the mnemonic device 'Every good boy does fine'. The spaces form the word 'FACE' and can be best remembered that way.

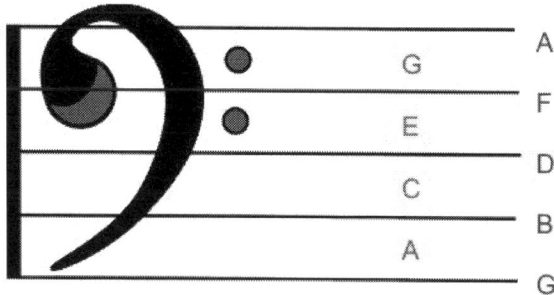

The F or bass, clef is located under the G clef, and it contains eight notes just like the G clef. The notes on the lines are G, B, D, F, and A, and the spaces are A, C, E, and G. The spaces form the word 'ACE' with a left over G, and the lines of the bass clef create the mnemonic 'Every Good Boy Deserves Fudge'.

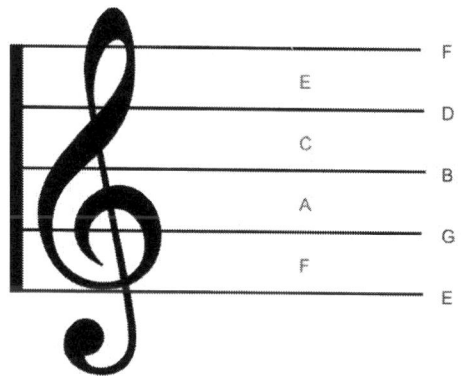

When more than two notes are played at the same time, they create something called a chord. When two notes are played together, they are called an interval. The most common type of chords in popular music are triads. Triads are just chords of three notes. Chords are created because they are notes with a similar pitch, and they all agree with each other. The name chord was actually derived from the accord, which means to be in agreement, or be harmonious. Just like song lyrics have song structure, there is a composition like this for a song's melody. This is called chord progression. Now, if you recall the study that was conducted in 2013 that asked songwriters how they began the songwriting process, there were some groups that weren't covered. One of these groups included songwriters that preferred to write chord progression first. This was actually the second largest group of songwriters, at 24%. If you don't remember, the group of songwriters that started with their lyrics was 36.5% large. The smallest group was another factor of melody - the beat. Only 5.5% of all questioned songwriters chose to start with the beat. Starting your song with a beat is difficult, and not recommended for beginners unless you already have a beat in mind. Chord progression is a great way to begin songwriting, especially if you don't want to start with the lyrics. But what is chord progression?

Chord progression is just a sequence of chords that move towards a certain key, or key while keeping harmony. Chords are notated by the use of Roman numerals. Each chord is assigned two Roman numerals for each key. One capital Roman numeral for the major chord, and one lowercase for the minor chord. Each chord is the Roman numeral I in its own key. So in the A key, A major would be I. B minor in A key would be ii. Chord progression is quite complicated, and a complete guide to chord progression can never be written due to the vast variety of chords. To further understand chord progression, you will need to independently research the topic. This book will provide some simple chord progressions that you can experiment with, however.

Progression	A	B	C	D	E	F	G
I - IV - V - V	A - D - E - E	B - E - F - F	C - F - G - G	D - G - A - A	E - F - B - B	F - G - C - C	G - A - D - D
I - I - IV - V	A - A - D - E	B - B - E - F	C - C - F - G	D - D - G - A	E - E - A - B	F - F - B - C	G - G - C - D
I - V - vi - IV	A - E - f - D	B - F - g - E	C - G - a - F	D - A - b - G	E - B - c - A	F - C - d - B	G - D - e - C
I - I - I - I	A - A - A - A	B - B - B - B	C - C - C - C	D - D - D - D	E - E - E - E	F - F - F - F	G - G - G - G
I - V - vi - iii	A - E - f - c	B - F - g - d	C - G - a - e	D - A - b - f	E - B - c - g	F - C - d - a	G - D - e - b
vi - V - IV - V	f - E - D - E	g - F - E - F	a - G - F - G	b - A - G - A	c - B - A - B	d - C - B - C	e - D - C - D
IV - iv - I	D - d - A	E - e - B	F - f - C	G - g - D	A - a - E	B - b - F	C - c - G
I - V - IV - V	A - E - D - E	B - F - E - F	C - G - F - G	D - A - G - A	E - B - A - B	F - C - B - C	G - D - C - D
I - IV - vi - V	A - D - f - E	B - E - g - F	C - F - a - G	D - G - b - A	E - A - c - B	F - B - d - C	G - C - e - D
I - IV - V	A - D - E	B - E - F	C - F - G	D - G - A	E - A - B	F - B - C	A - D - f - E

In the provided table, the chord progression is labeled 'progression' on the far left. These are the Roman numerals that denote the actual chords.

The letters on the right of the progression column signify the key that the letter represents. In the key columns, lowercase letters represent minor chords, and capital ones represent major chords. Hopefully, with the help of this chart, you understand the extremely complicated concept of chord progression a little better. If you don't understand it and it just looks like a jumble of letters, it's okay. A little research will clear that up, and you'll be playing these in no time. Once you get it, start playing around with a few of the chord progressions listed in the chart. These are beginner ones common in popular music. They sound great and aren't too hard to learn. If you want to use more complex ones, then you're free to as well.

Finalizing Your Song

Now your song is complete. You have it all on paper. But what can you do with a sheet of paper with some scribbles and chords written on it? You need to finalize your song and make it professional. Think of everything you've done so far as a rough draft. It's time to clean up the errors, dot your i's, and cross your t's. To beginning the process of finalizing your song, you need a sample audience. Close friends and family make the best first listener's because they will tell you their honest opinions. Make sure not to look to someone who sugar coats everything - at this point in the editing stage, all you need is the harsh truth. If the title needs revision, change it up a bit. If your lyrics sound too dull, add some flavor. You never want to go to a stranger or someone who is scared of hurting your feelings; otherwise you won't be able to receive honest feedback. Once you've selected a few people to listen to your song, you can play it to them live or record it on a something simple like a camera. For now, a crude video is fine.

 Once your feedback returns, use it. Don't get offended, the people that suggest revisions are actually the people trying to help you. Those that keep their mouth shut are hurting you more than they know. Once you fix up what you needed to, you've made it to homestretch. Now, you have to consider how you want to get your song out there. In the age of the internet, we have countless ways to publish and self-publish. You may utilize any of the hundreds of video and music sharing websites, or you may seek out a more professional route. You may even just record the song for yourself and friends. If you choose to put your song on a video sharing website, then you're going to need to do one last step. You need to find professional audio recording software to make your song professional. There are several free programs that specialize in this. One software to consider is Audacity, created by the Audacity Team. It's very simple and very effective. You don't need an all-out recording studio, but if you want to go all out, look into recording studios in your area. You may even want to build your own if you are looking to make songwriting your future. Some other great programs to check out are The LMMS Project, GarageBand, FL Studio, and Stagelight. Do some research on these programs, as some of them cost more than others and each have their strengths.

 Whether you decide to record your song professionally or not, you may want to play your song at concerts, parties, friend's house, or even just for fun. If you have the equipment, then this is great. If not, this isn't much of a problem. You can rent a microphone, guitar, and even something as large as a piano. Solo performances may seem even more daunting than when you have other people on the stage. You might want to add some more instruments to your melody, and get together a band. The most important thing to do when you're performing is to be confident in your work. Don't stress over the little things, and remember the amount of time you spent putting into your song. Practice, courage, and determination are great ways to eradicate the effects of stage fright. After all, if you know you spent two months practicing for this concert, what do you have to be afraid of? If you start getting nervous, instead of imagining people in their underwear, start thinking about the calm, quiet room you practiced in. Forget that there is a crowd, and just play your music. They do say ignorance is bliss!

Songwriting may become overwhelming so here's a checklist so that you can keep track of all your hard work!

- Research popular music

- Pick a genre, and do more research

- Decide whether to write the melody or lyrics first

- Free write to get started

- Create an interesting a title

- Write a catchy hook

- Research poetry and other literature

- Understand song structure

- Research your favorite songs' melodies

- Experiment with melodies by humming

- Learn some instrument basics

- Understand basic chord progressions

- Compose your melody

- Decide what to do with your music

- Continue writing music

Conclusion

Thank you again for downloading this book! I hope this book was able to help you to write amazing songs in a short amount of time.

Now you are a full-blown songwriter. After all the effort, research, time, and energy you put into it do you feel like it paid off? Do you believe that you could make this commitment again and write another song? If so, then you are a true songwriter. If you feel like it was just a one-time thing, that's okay too. Don't let the hard work scare you off, because it's a rewarding process. Some of us may think that something is our passion until we actually try it. At least you gave it a try. And for those that believe they have found their passion - keep writing music. You will get the hang of it the more you do it, and before you know it, all this work will become second nature. If you believe that you are on your way to becoming a songwriter professionally, then don't stop.

Finally, if you enjoyed this book, please take the time to share your thoughts and post a review on Amazon. It'd be greatly appreciated!

Thank you and good luck!

Check Out My Other Book

"How to Write a Song: Beginner's Guide to Writing a Song in 60 Minutes or Less"

copy this URL: http://amzn.to/1QOBrOU

Here is a quick preview of the introduction for you:

Many people have lifelong dreams of becoming rock stars, pop legends or folk hits but due to life's surprising nature, they never truly get a chance to achieve these feats. However, the craze of songwriting may not exit their minds throughout their life and at one point or another, it would become extremely hard for them to avoid the thought of writing their own song. Most of these people have never written a song ever in their lifetime and so are unaware of the entire process. They want to get started right away, skip the boring parts, for which they don't have time and get a song ready as quickly as possible. This is exactly what this book sets out to accomplish.

The book will teach you the basics of song writing and will cover all the aspects necessary for a well-structured song. It will provide you with techniques that will enhance your skills to such a level that you'll be able to write songs in under an hour!

You won't be disappointed!

Printed in Great Britain
by Amazon